Charles Redd Monographs in Western History

Charles Redd Monographs in Western History

No. 2

John M. Townley

Conquered Provinces: Nevada Moves Southeast, 1864-1871

The Charles Redd Monographs in Western History are made possible by a grant from Charles Redd. This grant served as the basis for the establishment of The Charles Redd Center for Western Studies at Brigham Young University.

PUBLISHED BY
BRIGHAM YOUNG UNIVERSITY PRESS
PROVO, UTAH 84602

ISBN: 0-8425-0417-6

Printed in the United States of America
Additional copies of this monograph or other numbers in this series may be purchased by writing to Brigham Young University, Marketing (University Press), 205 UPB, Provo, Utah 84602.
73 .85M 16173

Contents

Conquered Provinces: Nevada Moves Southeast, 1864-1871

John M. Townley

Introduction

In September 1865 a prospector working in the recently discovered Pahranagat district wrote to the Nevada governor requesting instructions for forming a county in that remote area. The letter was the opening shot in a dispute over the region that involved Nevada, Arizona, Utah, and the federal government for six years and ended only after the loss of sizable territories by Utah and Arizona, the mass abandonment of several settlements along the Muddy River, and the effective political subordination of the Latter-day Saint (Mormon) community in Meadow Valley. At the time, Pahranagat and all of southeastern Nevada were more than one hundred miles beyond the settlement line in the central and western portions of the state. At stake was the area comprising modern Lincoln and Clark counties, where the contending parties were the Mormon ranchers and the first wave of the expanding mining frontier.

Development of southeastern Nevada was primarily tied to Utah and the East. Most of the risk capital came from New York State, where the majority of companies were incorporated. The initial mineral discoveries were made by parties from either Salt Lake City or the "Dixie" settlements of southern Utah. While communication with Salt Lake City was routine, no one in 1865 had crossed the deserts separating Pahranagat from Carson City. Finally, any fair sampling of opinion would show that the majority of residents were satisfied with Utah's theodemocracy and low tax rates.

Yet, despite precedent and the wishes of the populace, the region was attached to Nevada. The reasons were largely economic, and an examination of those reasons forms the basis of this paper.

1. The Pahranagat Boom

Early Settlement of Southeastern Nevada

Permanent settlement of present-day Lincoln County, Nevada, resulted from the typical pioneer urge to exploit the natural resources of the region. Silver mineralization was discovered in late 1863 near modern Pioche, while the Francis Lee family arrived in Meadow Valley on May 4, 1864, hoping to convert the grassy bottomland into farms and cattle pastures.[1] At the time, Meadow Valley was still a no-man's-land between the rigidly structured society of Mormon Utah and the competitive, chaotic mining frontier pushing eastward from the Comstock Lode. Neither the discoverers of silver nor the Lee family saw themselves as antagonists; each wanted only to be left alone to develop the abundant resources of the area. However, men with more imagination were soon to become involved in this initial contact between two divergent societies. Had the region been barren of metals it would have remained a rural backwater, but silver was to be the catalyst that added another large geographical area to Nevada and brought it to its final boundaries.

The first visit to the silver outcrops near what was later to become Pioche, Nevada, was made by William Hamblin, an LDS missionary among the southern Utah Indians, between mid-1863 and March 1864. Hamblin was taken to the deposits by one of his Indian contacts but failed to erect claim monuments or organize a mining district. There is no evidence that he had mining experience or recognized the value of his find. Further, he may have visited the location as much as a year earlier. The *Deseret News* issue of June 22, 1864, included an editorial comment to the effect that the deposits had been known to the Mormons for a long period, then went on to depreciate the advantages of mining.[2] There is some corroborating evidence of an earlier discovery in a letter from El Dorado Canyon, a mining district on the Colorado River, stating that a party of miners from southern Nevada had found silver north of the Muddy River around 1863.[3] Hamblin himself claimed to have been aware of the deposits for at least two years prior to the establishment of a mining district in 1864.[4]

After returning from the Pioche region, Hamblin reported the discovery to Church officials. By February 1864, word of the silver deposits was common in Salt Lake City. In that month, a party of five gentile miners headed by Stephen Sherwood and J. N. Vandermark decided to prospect the southern Utah region. They first visited the Santa Clara settlements and then headed for Meadow Valley to find Hamblin.

Nine years later, the leaders of the prospecting party testified in litigation between the leading Pioche mining firm and one of its competitors.[5] The accounts of the trip varied somewhat, but the witnesses agreed that they found Hamblin on a ranch in Clover Valley, where he provided the party with directions to the outcrops. He may have agreed to meet them on the ground, but in any case, he was inspecting the deposits when the prospectors arrived on March 15 or 16, 1864.

Until March 18, the men prospected the immediate area of the outcrops and erected location markers. Then they held a formal meeting at Panaca Spring, organizing the Meadow Valley mining district. Hamblin acted as chairman and Sherwood was elected recorder. The district created was sixty miles square, and these first claims were known as the "Panaca ledge" until the boom period in 1869, when they became the property of the Raymond and Ely Company.[6]

The following day Hamblin returned to the locations, while Sherwood and Vandermark left for Salt Lake City. Before attempting to develop any of the claims, the men wanted to run assays on samples to determine which exposures were most valuable. Sherwood's party returned to the claims about June 1, 1864, and collected additional samples for a more comprehensive series of tests on the rock. During 1864 some 1,400 pounds of ore had been assayed, and the owners could produce verified assays that indicated values of up to $300 per ton for their discoveries.[7] With this evidence, Sherwood went east to raise capital for development of the deposits. While Sherwood and Vandermark were occupied with testing the claims, Hamblin built a small furnace near the exposures and attempted to smelt some of the richer rock. Sherwood later identified the site of the furnace as being "on the point of rocks north of Meadow Valley Street."[8]

The same rumors that interested Sherwood and Vandermark in southern Utah brought others into the area. This growing influx of prospectors alarmed local leaders of the LDS Church. They fully realized what the effect of a full-scale mining boom would be on the influence of the Church in Utah. At the same time, the Meadow Valley region was a political vacuum; to draw the line between Utah's church-dominated society and Nevada's lack of social stability in that area would encapsulate the threat to Mormon hegemony. Every attempt at coexistence in the development of the LDS Church had ended in disaster. The Mormons' escape into the Mountain West was intended to isolate themselves from persecution and build a new Zion in the wilderness. Now, seventeen years later, the enemy was again approaching. He was not just passing through on the road to California; he was looking for mineral deposits and intending to locate permanently in order to work them. Meadow Valley was the threshold to the older Utah towns; as such it must become the outer defense line for the Mormon commonwealth.

LDS tactics were simple and based on experience: they would occupy the arable lands, lay claim to all water rights, and deny the mineral deposits of the area to incoming gentiles by staking the outcrops. Erastus Snow, president of the Southern Utah Mission, visited Meadow Valley in May 1864 and recognized the growing outside interest. He sent additional colonists from southern Utah and authorized the Panaca residents to lay claim to the exposures discovered by Hamblin.[9] Without the spur of outside competition, it seems doubtful that southeastern Nevada would have been so quickly and methodically settled. There is probably a connection between the occupation of the Muddy Valley in 1865 by an LDS mission and the general policy to create a bulwark between older Utah settlements and the Nevada mining frontier.

The anticipated problems with gentile mining interests in

Meadow Valley were only illusory in 1864, however. A few prospecting parties drifted in and sampled the outcrops. General Patrick Edward Connor, commanding officer of the Union forces stationed in Utah, had a wagon road surveyed that connected Salt Lake City with Meadow Valley and the southern Utah settlements.[10] In anticipation of bringing immigrants and freight into Utah via the Colorado River, Brigham Young instructed Anson Call to select a point on the river as a steamboat landing and warehouse complex. This transportation center was to be connected with Salt Lake City by General Connor's road. Further, the Muddy Valley, located between Panaca and Call's Landing, was colonized in 1865. The expansion of LDS settlements in southern Utah and Nevada was intended to nullify the threat of gentile intrusion.[11]

But this supposed threat was more apparent than real. The ore exposed on the surface was too complex to be treated by the milling techniques available in 1864. In fact, over five years of work in other mining centers was required before a process was perfected that would economically separate the Meadow Valley silver. From 1864 until 1869, the Panaca ledge was almost forgotten by the mining industry, while the LDS Church administration prepared for a conflict in its southern territories by creating a buffer state.

Discovery and Early Development

The visits of Sherwood and Vandermark to Salt Lake City, accompanied by the assay reports on their samples, interested growing numbers of miners in the Meadow Valley region.[12] The party that located the Pahranagat district in early 1865 was acting on the rumors and other information that circulated in Salt Lake City concerning the possibilities of southern Utah as a mineral belt. Even more interesting is the possibility that influential LDS members, perhaps as high as First Presidency level, had conceived a policy of actively prospecting the area and locating the deposits in advance of the gentile miners. This policy could be implemented by sending parties of LDS members and sympathetic miners into the region. The mining

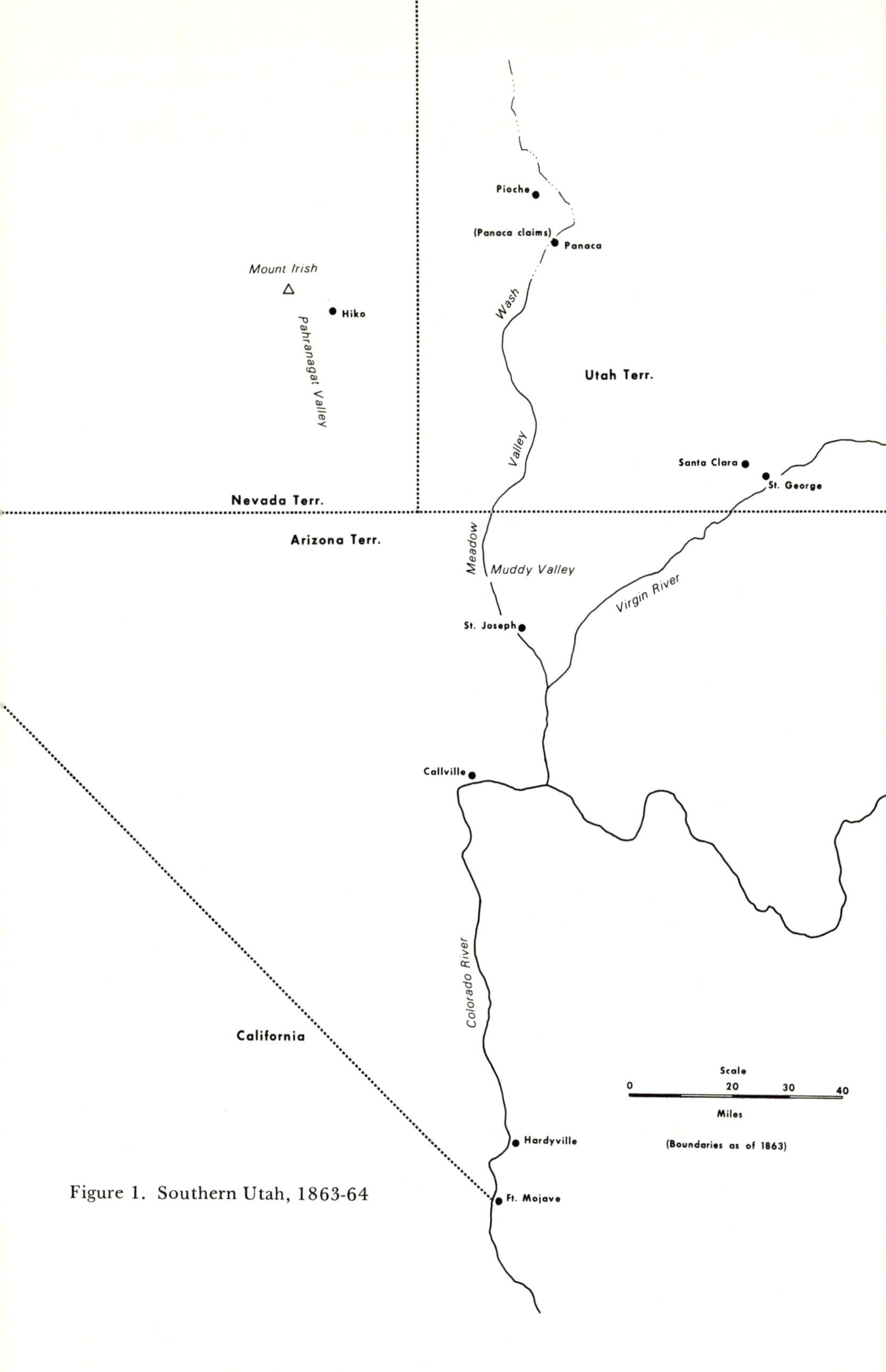

Figure 1. Southern Utah, 1863-64

expertise would be provided by the gentiles, while the Church could provide guides and assistance through the settlements in southern Utah. The advantages of this approach were quick assessment of the region's mineral potential and assurance that any favorable deposits would belong to LDS members or sympathizers.

The discovery of the Pahranagat district resulted from a cooperative prospecting venture such as proposed above. Like the earlier Sherwood-Vandermark party, this group originated in Salt Lake City. Attracted by the rumors prevalent in the Utah capital, they intended to search for minerals between St. George and the Colorado. John H. Ely, an experienced prospector who later married the daughter of a prominent family in Panaca, headed the party of six men. The guide and interpreter was Ira Hatch, LDS missionary and veteran of almost a decade in southern Utah exploration. Hatch was a deeply loyal member of the Church and would not have violated the injunction against mining unless instructed by higher authority. Leaving Salt Lake City in early 1865, they prospected the area north of Callville, using the LDS settlements as sources of supply. By early March they had worked their way from Callville to Panaca. While there, they were visited by an Indian from Pahranagat Valley who claimed to have knowledge of a mineral outcrop in that area. The prospectors followed the usual practice of carrying hand specimens of various ores to show the Indians living in the regions they visited, offering trade goods for information. Convinced that the Indian was in earnest regarding the ore sample, the party followed him to Pahranagat and on the seventeenth of March were led to a series of large silver outcrops, high on the east flanks of Mount Irish.[13] They spent three days in mapping the immediate area and recording their claims. Then, taking samples for analysis, they returned to Panaca.

The unusual regulations adopted by the original locators of the Pahranagat deposits support the LDS-gentile cooperative thesis suggested earlier. According to the district regulations, a single monument built of native stone entitled the locator to perpetual title.[14] This feature was a drastic departure from the

California and Nevada precedents. By 1865 the customary district regulations required, on penalty of forfeiting title, a specified amount of annual work and numerous monuments or corner posts on each claim. Continuity in mining district law was the norm; departures from previous experience were rare. The abandonment of the customary requirements in the Pahranagat district is difficult to excuse as simply a local aberration. Its usefulness to the first men on the ground seems the best explanation. Under the peculiar laws of the district they could easily monopolize the best properties, permanently hold title to the deposits, and deny the area to later arrivals. Further, by their choosing to let the properties remain undeveloped, there would be no reason for the influx of undesirables. The tactic of monopolizing the most valuable deposits seemed to be a solution to the fear of outside intrusion, since it could be used to prevent any development of the ore bodies and gave no reason for the mining fraternity to rush to areas where the best properties were held by others.

The Ely-Hatch party evidently returned to Salt Lake City from Panaca in late March 1865. Although the ores taken from the surface seemed rich, any experienced miner wanted confirmation from assays. These first tests must have been satisfactory, because the men returned in June. A month later they were forced from the area by threats from local Indians. Not until October did enough men gather in Meadow Valley to justify a return to the deposits, this time permanently.

Word of the Pahranagat discoveries spread quickly throughout the Mountain West. By the fall months of 1865 over one hundred men were prospecting the slopes of Mount Irish. The surface indications had convinced many men, often in high political and business circles, that a broad belt of silver ore stretched southeast from the Comstock, through Austin and Belmont, to Pahranagat. Opportunity for fabulous riches, similar to the experience on the Comstock, could be found in Pahranagat, but the race was to the swift.

As the news from Mount Irish followed the usual pattern of being exaggerated completely beyond the bounds of probability, Nevada politicians began to see advantages of incorporating the district into their new state. The opportunity may have been suggested by a Pahranagat miner in a letter to Governor Henry Goode Blasdel, written in midsummer 1865:

> *James M. Day writes to Governor Blasdel, from Salt Lake City, a letter descriptive of a new mining region, which he supposes to be in the southeastern corner of Nevada. The letter is published in the Carson* Appeal, *which paper supposes the new mines to be in Utah and not in Nevada. The mines are in what is called the Pahranagat Lake District, and about 120 miles from Call's Steamboat Landing, on the Colorado river. Day speaks of the mines as being rich in silver, and asks for information from the Governor in regard to the proper steps to be taken for the organization of a county.*[15]

By the late fall months, a small-scale "rush" to Pahranagat had brought men from Nevada, Utah, and Arizona to the district to test its promise. At least one eastern promoter had been sufficiently interested to visit the deposits and had returned to New York City determined to incorporate the properties he had bonded.[16]

The politicians were scarcely less active than the prospectors. Nevada's congressional delegation had been instructed to enter a bill moving the state's eastern boundary another degree of longitude into the Territory of Utah. This alteration of the border would remove the doubt about Pahranagat's location; it would be firmly included in a mining state and free from the domination of the religious fanatics of Utah (at least so ran the arguments). Thus within nine months the pattern of the Nevada-Utah dispute was set: Nevada claimed to be a progressive state that could provide the most favorable framework for mining activity, while Utah allegedly remained a bigoted backwater unable to move with the times. Congress would best serve the interests of the West by enlarging Nevada to include these prospective bonanzas, which could be exploited under the enlightened administration of Carson City. The claims of Utah to the territory, based on discovery and the wishes of the majority of the inhabitants, were ignored.[17] A Congress that was treating the ex-Confederate states as conquered provinces was even less delicate with the territories of Utah and Arizona. Not content with taking another degree of longitude from Utah, Congress also enlarged Nevada to the south by giving her access to the Colorado River.[18] The Radical Republican need for Nevada's congressional votes justified this *quid pro quo*. Had Utah or Arizona been beyond the territorial stage of political development, this unjust geographical vivisection would have been impossible. However, territories were creatures of the Congress, and the bill signed on May 5, 1866, is an example of how they could be manipulated for larger ends. Nevada's ability to provide senatorial votes for party legislation enabled her to obtain favorable action on the boundary question. Her final limits were determined by the president's signature to Senate Bill No. 155, effective May 5, 1866. The Nevada legislature confirmed the cession by formal resolution on January 18, 1867.[19]

Once potentially profitable mineral deposits had been located in the unmapped areas between Utah and Nevada, it was inevitable that Nevada assume sovereignty over the districts. Despite the LDS effort to deny the deposits to outsiders by monopolizing ownership among Church members or sympathizers, they could never develop effective counterarguments to the charge that the Church-dominated Utah government was against mining activity on ethical grounds. Brigham Young was often quoted on the subject:

> *"Gentlemen," said he, "I understand some of you are going to the Pahranagat mines. You are very hopeful, I observe, but you will lose your money. . . . Set one hundred men to mining and ten to farming, and at the end of ten years the ten will be worth more than the one hundred, and probably have to feed them gratuitously."*[20]

Numerous personal comments such as this, coupled with the continual propaganda printed in the *Deseret News* and the *Salt Lake Daily Telegram*, newspapers following Church policy, gave the Nevada politicians ready-made excuses to extend the

Map of the Pahranagat silver mines, from W. H. Mills, *Columbia Silver Mining Company* (New York: Office of the "Pacific Index," 1865), folded map.

mining-centered Nevada government over any subsequent mineral discovery. The First Presidency was on the horns of a painful dilemma: it had to fight the tendency of members to move to the attractive mining boom towns but feared the movement of the mining frontier toward the central Church settlements along the Wasatch front. To work openly toward a compromise with mining interests would weaken its hold on members and risk breaking up the purely agricultural Utah commonwealth. At length the Church abandoned its policy of monopolizing the new discoveries in Utah's southwestern regions and placed mining beyond the pale.[21]

2. The Boom Peaks

Two years were required for the Pahranagat excitement to reach its peak. Overly optimistic information concerning the district began to spread in midsummer 1865, bringing several hundred men from surrounding camps into the region. The very remoteness of the discovery added romance and mystery to its potential. A series of corporations was formed in New York City and other eastern centers; funds from these investors kept activity high until the summer months of 1867. In order to make the district more attractive to out-of-state investors, county government was instituted by the creation of Lincoln County in February 1866.

The last half of 1865 appears to have been a period of steady increase in numbers of white residents in Pahranagat Valley and on Mount Irish. The better mineral locations were discovered quickly and camps grew up near them. On the east side of Mount Irish were Logan Springs, the best source of water in the area, and Silver Canyon, located nearest the principal mines. Logan Springs remained the largest settlement during the boom period; its source of water caused most of the smelters and mills built on Mount Irish to be located there. On the west side of the mountain, a camp grew up about Hatfield's Springs. Discoveries of silver in the List ledge led to the erection of a mill at the springs, and the camp assumed the name of Crescent City. These three camps remained the centers for development and transportation until the district collapsed in 1869.

The usual officers necessary for a mining district were apparently elected in the fall months of 1865. The sheriff, George Rogers, was later killed by Indians. Most claim holders chose to spend their time in prospecting rather than developing their properties. Many intended to sell their claims to companies that could fully exploit the deposits. There seems to have been no hesitancy on the part of the earliest locators to sell their claims, or at least to bond their properties to promoters. Mineralization seemed to occur along a five-mile exposure of quartz ledges. The major properties—the Illinois, Indiana, and Webster claims—were located on what was called the Hiko vein. The vein had numerous cross-faults, which were named for various individuals, but the only significant ore bodies were within the main mineral channel. These large ore bodies were claimed by the first group of miners to visit the area in March 1865. They were later bonded to William Henry Raymond and became the chief assets of the companies he organized in New York City early in 1866.

Like the Comstock, Pahranagat was to be owned by out-of-state capital. However, in this instance the outside source was east of the Mississippi, not San Francisco. The largest of these companies was the International Silver Mining Company, owner of the Illinois and Indiana claims and some 20,000 feet of other claims in the district. This firm and the Pahranagat Valley Silver Mining Company were organized and administered by Raymond. Employing another of the Comstock's devices, Raymond used the Pahranagat Valley Silver Mining Company as the parent firm for all milling work. Raymond visited Pahranagat in late 1865, bonded the best properties, then traveled directly to New York City, where he incorporated the above companies for mining speculation. While on Mount Irish, Raymond met John H. Ely, who had led the discovery party to the district and held the claims that Raymond bonded. For the next decade, the two men would be associated in the development of southeastern Nevada's mineral resources.

While Raymond was spending the first half of 1866 in the East, influential figures in Nevada and Utah were assessing Pahranagat's potential and taking options on claims that could, hopefully, be sold to investors. The most active of these individuals was Henry G. Blasdel, governor of Nevada. He worked at two levels: creating local government for Lincoln County, and forwarding information to prospective investors in Pahranagat silver properties. Like Raymond, he was in contact with John Ely regarding his discoveries.[22] Governor Blasdel was sufficiently intrigued with the possibilities that he traveled cross-country from Carson City to Pahranagat in the spring of

1866.[23] The ostensible reason given was to take a census of the residents of the district in order to create the new county government. However, it is difficult to rationalize why the governor of the state felt called upon to perform a task better left to a clerk. Further, the presence in the party of the state mineralogist and members of the legislature suggests that all concerned were interested in personally assessing the new bonanzas for possible investment. Blasdel's party could not find enough voters to institute the proposed county but did open a wagon route between Pahranagat and Austin that eventually became the principal supply and stage route.

Utah's public servants beat Governor Blasdel to the new silver district. A letter from Pahranagat dated May 20, 1866, discusses Governor Charles Durkee's offer of $8,000 for a part interest in the Green Monster claim.[24] Earlier, a Salt Lake City newspaper had included a statement that "Governor Durkee will go on to the Pahranagat mines after transacting his business at Fort Ephraim."[25] Durkee probably beat Blasdel by less than two weeks. The Nevada party arrived on May 15, and the Utah representatives had departed by that time.

Indian problems developed as more miners entered the district. The band of Paiutes that occupied Pahranagat Valley could not be expected long to tolerate the preemption of their irrigated plots and meadowlands. On March 1, 1866, George Rogers, sheriff of the district, was killed as he rode between Hiko and Panaca. One of the Indians involved was captured at Panaca and taken to Hiko by Judge John S. Atchison. The Indian "was given a fair trial and then hung" by the miners.[26] This occasion may have been the first contact between John Ely and the Atchison family. Two or three years later, Ely married Emma Atchison and worked closely with the Panaca residents, despite remaining outside the LDS faith.[27] Both the Pahranagat and Panaca communities suffered from Indian raids, and lone prospectors were often fired upon while they were working. The conflict was settled by massive retaliation on the Indians, after which the bands maintained a sullen dependency on the settlements.[28]

The men who flocked to Pahranagat in late 1865 and early

1866 were the first to become disillusioned. Many were from central Nevada, and they wrote to the *Reese River Reveille* explaining conditions as they saw them:

> *I will give you my opinion of this country by saying we are beautifully bilked. There is not a mine here that I would have as a gift. . . . You remember a piece of ore that was shown to us and others in Austin as coming from this district; well, I am now satisfied that it came from the Gould and Curry mine.*[29]

Although the assays made indicated several hundred dollars in silver to the ton of selected rock, there was no production from the district during the first five months. The men holding the better claims hoped to sell out quickly and did nothing to improve their properties other than remove some of the overburden to expose the vein for inspection. Without underground exploration, the ultimate value of the deposits was still uncertain.

In late spring, agents representing eastern corporations arrived to operate their properties and build the first crude milling facilities. Dr. O. H. Congar and Captain Dahlgren appear to have arrived in early June.[30] Both men brought equipment with them to erect smelters. Logan Springs was selected as the site for experimentation because of its water.[31] Slag from the small smelting furnaces can still be seen there. Dr. Congar also had a stamp mill ordered, to be shipped via the Colorado River.[32] The arrival of these worthies gave a boost to the waiting district. They hired men to open claims and cast brick for their furnaces. The intrusion of capital created another blaze of optimism.

The return of Henry Raymond in August with the first stamp mill was a decisive event in the progress of the camp.[33] Representing several New York companies with full treasuries, Raymond quickly became the leading figure on Mount Irish. The remaining months of 1866 flew by in a rush as Raymond hired dozens of men to stockpile ore from the Illinois mine and prepare a millsite near Hiko for his five-stamp experimental mill. At the same time, San Francisco merchants were building a warehouse at Callville to contain the merchandise they hoped to distribute in southeastern Nevada and Utah.[34] Traffic into Pahranagat became so heavy during the summer that a stage line between Salt Lake City and Hiko was established, the trip taking five days and costing $75 one way.[35] Access was still difficult from the west; a California prospecting party had to fight its way into the district through deserts and Indians.[36]

By November, Raymond's mill was ready to operate. Ore had been brought down from the Illinois mine and dumped next to the stamps. Most of November and December were consumed in the initial attempt to separate the silver values. The mill first worked the ore by the wet method but freed only twenty percent of the assay value. Deciding to roast the ore prior to separation, Raymond had a small furnace built. Neither method worked satisfactorily.[37] The final *filip* came when the stamp mill drove its battery box out of sight in the soft valley mud. The mill was shut down in January; reduction could wait until Raymond's ten-stamp mill arrived from the Colorado River. None of the milling facilities built in 1866 satisfactorily worked the Pahranagat ores.

By the beginning of 1867, six to eight incorporated firms were conducting mining operations in the district, in addition to numerous small groups of miners. A wagon road between Austin and Hiko had opened along the route taken by Governor Blasdel in 1866, and the district was far less remote than a year earlier. Although no production had yet been generated from Pahranagat, several hundred residents were spread between Hiko and the claims on Mount Irish. Miners and suppliers were optimistic enough to accept promissory notes from the companies in lieu of cash.[38]

Another prominent personage made Pahranagat his headquarters in 1866. Evidently intrigued by his conversations with Governor Blasdel in Death Valley during April, C. C. Breyfogle, supposed discoverer of a fabulous gold mine in southern Nevada, drifted into Hiko later in the year. Breyfogle succeeded in raising a grubstake from the Pahranagaters and interested a party of nine men in returning to Death Valley to search for his lost mine.[39] He returned from that trip, perhaps wiser but no richer, in time to join William Hamblin and another group heading for the Grand Canyon to prospect for gold placers. Hamblin was the discoverer of the Pioche claims and evidently was continuing to prospect the southern Utah region. In December the party left Hiko for the Colorado. Several small placers were found, but Breyfogle was wounded in a skirmish with the Hualapais, some seventy-five miles upstream from Callville.[40] Men from Austin, who knew Breyfogle when he was operating a boardinghouse there in 1864, saw the local celebrity in Hiko while he was recuperating.[41] After this trip, Breyfogle abandoned Pahranagat for more promising fields of opportunity.

The first half of 1867 was dominated by the activities of the Crescent Silver Mining Company, a New York firm whose agent was Julius A. Bidwell. The company was a near-perfect example of the way capital was raised in the East, entrusted to inexperienced hands, then quickly squandered, leaving the investors with a few worthless claims and an inoperative mill. Incorporation of the firm was recorded in October 1866, whereupon the new agent called upon the *American Journal of Mining* editor to discuss his plans. The interview revealed the usual competence of eastern agents:

> *He owns one-tenth of the stock and appears to be a very nice gentleman, but when he called on us last week, and we asked him: "What mine have you ever worked in or superintended?" He answered: "None—I'm quite new in the business."*[42]

Mr. Bidwell was to get an education before he was through.

The major asset of the Crescent organization was a claim on the List ledge. This property was on the west side of Mount Irish and rested undiscovered until long after the lodes on the eastern slopes had been developed. An Indian revealed the outcrop, and the claims made by a Mr. List became parts of the Crescent Company's holdings.[43] Agent Bidwell arrived in the winter of 1867 and promptly became associated with O. H. Congar, agent for the Alameda Company, which owned claims

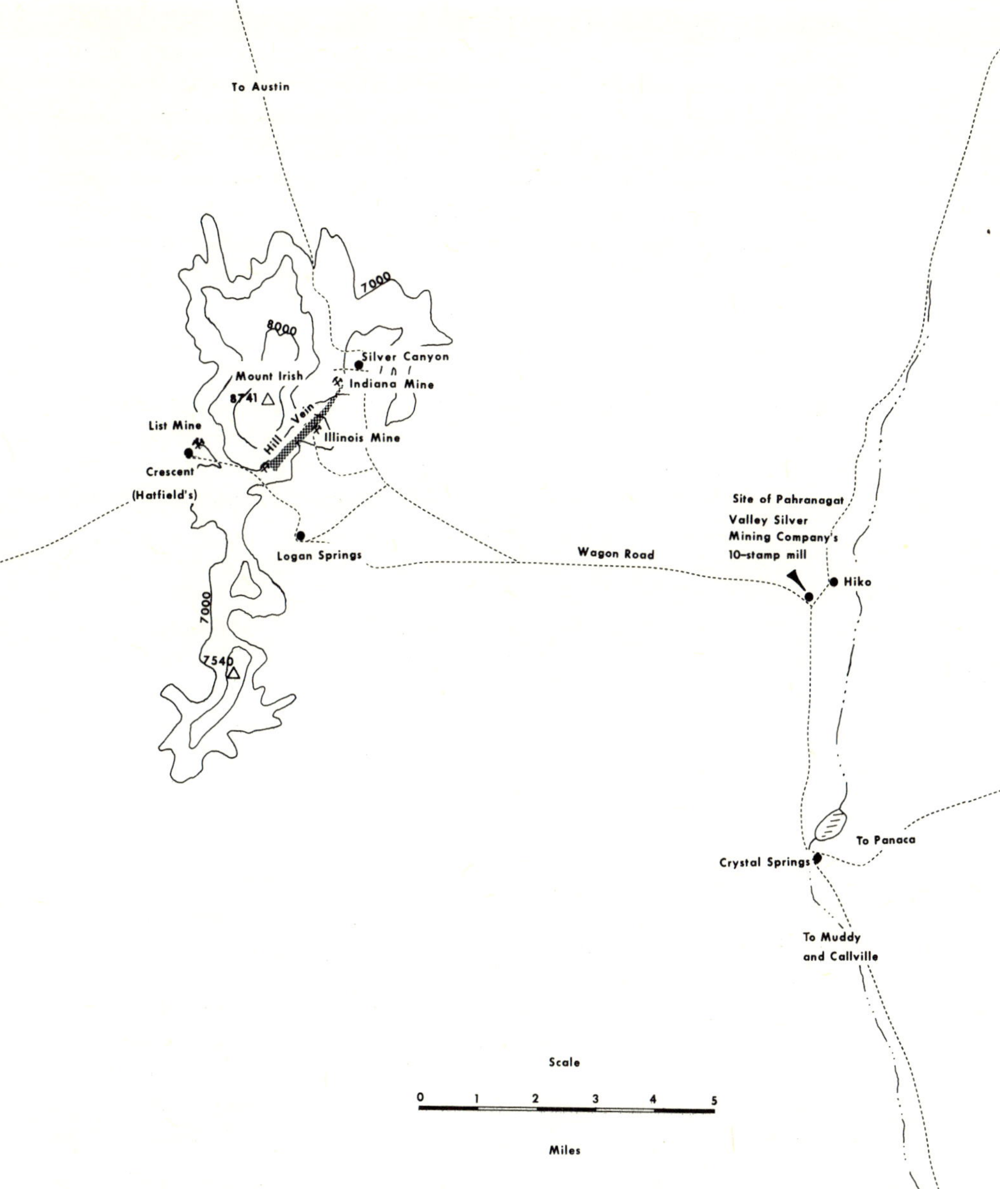

Figure 2. Pahranagat District, 1865-71

adjoining the Crescent properties on the List lode. Bidwell had ordered a five-stamp mill, with amalgamating equipment, all of which was delivered to Hatfield's Springs, only a mile from the mine, where water for milling was sufficient. Bidwell hired large crews to assemble the mill, build a wagon road over the pass between Logan Springs and Crescent City, and remove ore from the mine. Initially, cash was paid to the miners and laborers, although by the summer the customary promissory note succeeded coin of the realm. However, the quality of rock in the List mine, combined with Bidwell's optimism and promises, persuaded miners and merchants to take the gamble.

Bidwell seems never to have sent samples of the rock outside the district for assay. He was determined to push his project quickly and begin shipping bullion in order to pay for development from production. The result was to deplete the company treasury, build up an overwhelming debt, and risk the whole enterprise on a single trial run of the mill.

The gamble ended as might be expected:

> *The new mill at Crescent City (Hatfield's) was set in motion and kept at work for about ten days on ore from the List lode . . . but as the entire structure had been put up on credit, a suspension was necessary, and it is now locked up and will remain so until money arrived to liquidate the indebtedness against it.*[44]

Neither the Crescent Company nor Bidwell could salvage anything from the ruins. But the failure affected more than a single company; the credit of the other operators was suspect. Miners and merchants became cautious and activity dropped to near zero.

The first cloud on Pahranagat's optimistic horizon had been the failure of Henry Raymond to find a means of working the local ores with his small mill in January 1867. Raymond, his millwright Crippen, and John Ely had gone to Salt Lake City in late January. Raymond sent a series of telegrams to his sponsors in New York City explaining the circumstances and asking for additional funds.[45] Ely had received $55,000 for his claims, most probably from Raymond's companies. He went east, bought a complete stock of general merchandise, and returned some months later to Hiko, where he entered a trade safer than mining promotion.[46]

Nothing daunted by his initial failure in milling Pahranagat ore, Raymond arranged shipment of a large ten-stamp mill from El Dorado Canyon, via Callville, to Hiko. The mill had been ordered in March 1866 and was not brought upstream to the canyon until October. Parts of the plant were still being landed by paddlewheelers the following January. Freight from the Colorado to Hiko ran twelve cents per pound.[47]

Arranging for shipment of the ten-stamp mill from the Colorado seems to have been Raymond's last act as agent for the Pahranagat Valley Silver Mining Company. Promises were unsuitable substitutes for ore shipments; when the board of directors learned of the failure of the milling plant, Raymond was replaced by James Ostrom. Ostrom must have arrived in the late spring of 1867, since major changes in policy are recorded in the media by June. Raymond remained in the area, however, and maintained his position as a leading figure. Other eastern firms used his services and provided him with an income.

Another firm was trying during the winter of 1867 to install a mill on its property. The Alameda Silver Mining Company had arranged for its five-stamp plant to be freighted over the Old Spanish Trail from Los Angeles to the Muddy, then north to Hiko. Delivery was delayed when the stock belonging to the teamsters was stolen by Indians at Las Vegas. The teamsters tracked the raiders to the Amargosa River but never recovered an animal.[48]

The costly business of finding a proper milling technique seems to have been at the bottom of the depression at Pahranagat in midsummer 1867. Eastern investors were not prepared to finance unproductive enterprises, and nothing had been produced in Pahranagat except assays and expenditures. The failure of Raymond's and Bidwell's milling plants dried up the source of capital. The miners and local merchants had been accepting promises and were willing to continue so long as there appeared any reasonable chance to collect from the companies. A wholesale replacement in agents resulted from the setbacks. Not until new representatives arrived from the East could the district resume its development.

3. Pahranagat's Decline

Once the flow of capital from outside investors subsided, local individuals lost no time in blaming the district's problems on the agents who had been lauded earlier for their enterprise and largesse. It is easier to find fault with methods and procedures than admit that the ore might be low-grade or too complex to be worked by the simple metallurgical processes available. When Henry Raymond left the district for a business trip to the East, the *Reese River Reveille* commented acidly:

> *Raymond and Conger have also gone east, and it is a matter of indifference to nearly all the people there whether they ever return or not. . . . It is true they have disbursed hundreds of thousands of dollars in various projects, and experiments, but it would puzzle any one to mention their first success or to name a single ledge they had fairly prospected.*[49]

The attitude of many Pahranagaters was expressed in a letter to the Belmont paper:

> *The cause of the dullness is about this: the Eastern operators here who have possession of the mines are a set of arrant humbugs. For a long time (as long at least as they would stand the press) they kept the miners at work upon tick. When this failed, they finally dispersed a little money to the workmen as an inducement to continue their labor.*[50]

This search for a scapegoat occurred in many Nevada mining districts. It followed a similar pattern: outside investment was welcomed so long as money was dispersed freely; if the district failed, then the agents were reviled for "ruining" the area.

All of the sources of information agree on one point: during the summer of 1867 the district lost population as miners reacted to the dull economic situation by leaving for more active camps. Only the Pahranagat Valley Silver Mining Company and the Alameda Silver Mining Company appear to have kept men employed during the summer. The other firms suspended operations and laid off their crews.[51] James Ostrom, the new agent for the PVSMC, recognized that until the district could begin shipping bullion its only record potential investors could consult was one of failure. A ten-stamp mill was stored in Hiko; by placing it in operation Ostrom could fully test the local ores by different techniques. This task occupied the leading company for the next two years.

Ostrom hired Benjamin Evans to design the proposed mill and get it in operation.[52] Evans was one of the most experienced mining engineers in the state and had built two of the largest mills erected in Nevada: the Twin River and Silver Peak plants. Both were isolated districts, like Pahranagat, and the decision shows that Ostrom was reacting to the comment that outside companies never utilized the experience that was available in Nevada.

Evans chose to place the mill a short distance to the west of the site of Raymond's five-stamp experimental plant. By moving to a higher position on the flanks of the valley, Evans was able to avoid the soft, marshy bottomland but still be close to the water needed for processing the ore.[53] Financing problems plagued construction; at one point Evans threatened to resign unless the home office paid the workmen.[54] By November the buildings and equipment had been completed, but some additional castings had to be fabricated in the Pioneer Foundry at Austin. These were delivered in January 1868 and the mill began crushing ore in April.[55] The first run lasted only a few days, for the brick made from local clay could not withstand the high temperatures of the furnace. The arches failed and had to be replaced.[56] However, the short period of operation had at least one advantage; the first silver bricks from Pahranagat arrived in Austin, by stage, in early May.[57] Ostrom traveled east to explain the problems involving the mill and was replaced by the firm.[58] Job security among agents for

Pahranagat mining enterprises resembled that enjoyed by the favorites of Catherine the Great.

Despite the many disappointments, the PVSMC was determined to carry on. The new agent, James Wilson, was furnished with ample funds to rectify problems with the mill and to improve the Indiana and Illinois mines. He built a tramway to bring ore down the hillside to a loading chute in the canyon below the Illinois workings.[59] Efforts were made in 1868 and 1869 to find a source of artesian water near the mines so that ore could be worked on Mount Irish and the twelve-mile haul to Hiko for milling could be eliminated.[60] While most other organizations were content to suspend work, PVSMC continued to invest funds in proving Pahranagat's potential, or lack of it.

The only other organization to continue actively after 1867 was the Alameda Company, with William Fleming as agent. Their efforts were restricted to the west side of Mount Irish, where they continued to open the List ledge. They obtained the defunct Crescent Company's mill, probably through sheriff's sale, and added their own five-stamp mill to the plant.[61] Julius Bidwell had remained in the district after the Crescent mill had been padlocked. He was to be connected with the mill for the next five years as superintendent and deputy sheriff. Fleming worked the List ore in the smelters ex-agent Congar had erected in Logan Springs, and occasionally delivered small amounts of bullion and salt from the Muddy Valley to Austin.[62]

Fleming's tenure as agent was short-lived; he was replaced by B. F. Dalton in early 1868. Soon thereafter Dalton's house in Hiko was burned by persons unknown.[63] Support for the new agent was minimal, and he had difficulties in keeping the company credit high enough to procure groceries for his crews from Hiko merchants.[64]

The Pahranagat district was quickly forgotten by Nevada's mining industry after 1867. The population declined from the peak of several hundred to probably less than one hundred by 1868. The exodus began in 1867, when men took their wages from the New York companies and left for the new placer discoveries at Tuscarora—or "Goose," as it was often called.[65] The men employed by the few remaining firms dropped tools and left in a unit when news of White Pine reached the district in 1868.[66] The growing excitement over Pioche in 1869 claimed those who headed toward southeastern Nevada in that year. Pahranagat had been tested and found wanting.

Hiko, the Metropolis of Pahranagat Valley

The first settlement in the valley appears to have been made in the fall of 1865, near Crystal Springs. When the legislation establishing Lincoln County was prepared in Carson City during February 1866 the county seat was placed there. The governor and other individuals had corresponded with John Ely, and the decision to place the county seat at Crystal Springs reflected the situation at the time. Settlement there is logical, since the most direct route from Panaca to Mount Irish passes the springs, then follows a still-visible wagon road to the mines.

On March 18, 1867, Hiko was named as the county seat. In the year between formation of the county and the change in location of the county seat, most of the valley residents had moved six miles north of Crystal Springs to the meadows surrounding Hiko. The reasons for the move are unclear: the irrigation system built by the Pahranagat band of Paiutes may have been preempted; or perhaps Raymond decided to erect his five-stamp mill in that location, and the residents chose to satellite themselves on the largest and best financed mining operation in the district. Access to the mines is no easier from Hiko, and the distance is approximately equal to that from Crystal Springs.

By the spring of 1866, less than a year after the discovery of silver, all irrigable land within Pahranagat Valley had been claimed.[67] Farmers and ranchers were quick to see the possibilities of marketing farm products to a booming mining district. Provisions and forage were scarce and expensive; the early settlers turned water on the land and planted crops. While a few visits were made by LDS groups, none settled. Panaca was the closest Mormon community and there was no attempt to establish a mission in the valley.

Hiko developed slowly. It was the remotest county seat in

the state and could be reached only by way of Utah or Arizona. The first stage line originated in Salt Lake City and offered service beginning in the summer of 1866. A post office was established at the same time, but mail to Austin and other Nevada communities was carried by Indian runners, not the U.S. mails.[68] Not until a stage line was established between Belmont and Hiko in June 1867 was mail delivered directly.[69]

The first name given the small community was Lawrence, the name of the initial postmaster.[70] It lasted for a year until the Paiute word *Hiko,* usually translated as "white man's town," replaced the earlier title. Even then, various spellings—e.g., *Hico, Hicko*—were found in the literature until late 1867, when *Hiko* gained general acceptance.[71]

Pahranagat was tied to Utah and the East for operating capital and supplies until mid-1867. In late 1866 men began to travel directly to Austin over a good wagon route.[72] Once this road became familiar, the cheapest means of bringing manufactured goods to Hiko was via Austin by wagon. Thereafter the *Reese River Reveille* carried frequent notices of shipments to Pahranagat and deliveries of farm produce from Utah to central Nevada by Mormon farmers who used the new road.[73] As the demand for produce in Pahranagat dwindled with the fortunes of the mining companies, Hiko residents began to ship their excess crops north. There was probably more profit made on Pahranagat Valley watermelons than all the silver shipped from the district.[74]

Hiko had its share of frontier violence. The first problems were associated with the local Indian band. The Indian farms were casually appropriated by the newcomers, who ran off the former owners at gunpoint. Reaction was swift and consisted primarily in murdering lone miners or sniping at travelers. In response, the residents of Hiko and Panaca seized several Indians unlucky enough to be in the settlements when news of a miner's death arrived, and hanged them out of hand. This predilection for instant retribution and the rapid growth of the white population convinced the Pahranagats that they had no option but to submit. Thereafter, they followed the usual practice of living off the mining camps by begging, a little day labor, and widespread petty theft.

The Pahranagat Valley was the scene of one of the most celebrated murders in frontier Nevada history. Until 1867 Hiko had been spared the usual inundation of gunmen and self-styled toughs. Then, in May, Sam Vail and Robert Knox drove a herd of several hundred half-broken ponies into the valley from Belmont. They rested the herd near Ash Springs for several weeks. Then, in early June, some Paiutes brought a saddle into Hiko to trade for food. The sheriff thought they may have stolen it and asked them to take him to where they said it had been found. The saddle had been uncovered by coyotes in the camp of Vail and Knox; the Indians had seen it while passing through and hoped to be able to use it for trade. The sheriff was taken to the camp, and in digging below where the saddle had been buried, he found the body of Knox, murdered by a blow that crushed the skull.

Vail had driven the herd into Utah a few days earlier but was captured near Austin. His attorney argued knowingly that to return him to Hiko for trial would be, for Vail, tantamount to suicide, since the residents had already made up their minds on the case. When the citizens of Hiko agreed in writing to give Vail a fair trial, however, the counselor approved Vail's transfer from the Austin jail to Hiko.

The attorney's fears proved all too correct. When Vail and a deputy sheriff arrived in Logan Springs on July 10, 1867, word was quickly brought to Hiko. The next morning most of the male residents rode to Logan Springs, took the prisoner, and brought him to Hiko, where he was given his fair trial and speedily hanged at 10:00 p.m. that evening.

There are reasons for the stern administration of justice in Hiko. It seems that after Vail murdered his partner, he buried the body and Knox's personal effects in the middle of camp, then spread his bedroll over the grave and slept there for a week or so. Cashier's checks and personal mail addressed to Knox were found in Vail's possession. The Hikoans were incensed at the crime and wanted to discourage other bravos from cluttering the streets of their fair community.[75]

One other killing disturbed the even tenor of the town: in March 1868 two partners in a faro and monte bank disagreed over the distribution of winnings and one partner was disemboweled with a skinning knife.[76] After 1868 Hiko was so ignored by the state press that altercations received little notice.

At its height Hiko may have contained two hundred residents, including those on nearby ranches, but from mid-1867 this total declined. The major residents were connected with either mining or county government. A brewery was about the only local industry. Although gold was discovered some two miles east of town, it never became important to local residents.

At its best, Hiko was hardly a preferable residence for anyone who could find any excuse to return to civilization. The summers were particularly bad, as a letter to Belmont indicates:

> *And then, what with the thermometer 110° in the shade and the atmosphere black with flies, with nothing but board shanties to sit in, while people around them get beastly drunk and roll themselves into convenient places in a ditch which flows past to escape the torments, won't they have a nice time? Yet such at present is a sketch of Pahranagat life. I say, d--n Pahranagat.*[77]

Still, life went on. The celebrations of the Fourth of July were always events of great magnitude. There was even a Hiko Glee Club that performed at the slightest excuse.

By 1869 work in the mines on Mount Irish had almost ceased through lack of interest by outside capital, and there were few miners left to employ had the opportunity been present. The remoteness of the area was shown by a scale of $6.50 per day for ordinary labor.[78] Only the PVSMC's mill was operating and shipping bullion. The extent of the exodus to other camps can be seen in the number of votes cast in the 1870 elections: only twenty-three.[79] The condition of Hiko was aptly described by the state mineralogist:

> *Hiko City, formerly the county seat, has not increased in size or population for several years. It is more especially noted for its swarms of mosquitos than for its activity and business prospects.*[80]

4. Final Political Settlement in Lincoln County

New Interest in Panaca

While the interest of Nevada's mining industry was fixed on Pahranagat, the Panaca claims slumbered unmolested. Indeed, the hopes that the deposits might prove barren grew each year as development stagnated. The LDS barrier of settlements from Meadow Valley to the Muddy increased in population and remained unchallenged by the mining frontier that now rested only sixty miles to the west. From 1864 until 1869 the markets created in Pahranagat and central Nevada for the excess produce of "Dixie" created a sense of optimism that argued for peaceful coexistence. Thus far, President Young's policy of monopolizing the natural resources of the border corridor between Utah and Nevada had proven out in practice. The Mormon and gentile communities still were firmly segregated, and apparently there was no pressure in Nevada to intrude into Meadow Valley or along the Muddy.

Events in central Nevada and the foreseen completion of the transcontinental railroad ultimately led to renewed interest in the Panaca claims. The complexity of the ores in Meadow Valley had been tested by many parties between 1864 and 1868, without any success. The Comstock veins had been high in silver and gold and low in the base metals. As the mining frontier moved eastward from Virginia City, the percentage of base metals increased. The Washoe Pan Process failed to work those ores with higher amounts of lead or zinc, such as were found at Eureka or Potosi. The White Pine ores were so rich in silver that constant experimentation finally resulted in the development of a smelting method that released the silver as well as the base metals. As descriptions of these small smelters were circulated in the mining periodicals, a few mining figures remembered the lead-rich deposits that had been ignored earlier, and sent representatives to those areas to tie up the better properties. The first experiments with the ores at Eureka were successful, and thoughtful men began to reevaluate other districts. One of these individuals with a sensitive anticipation for profit was F. L. A. Pioche of San Francisco.

Pioche reacted to the new developments in the Nevada mining scene by sending Charles E. Hoffman to Panaca in 1868.[81] Hoffman's sponsor was a near-Renaissance man in the turbulent San Francisco of the 1860s. He was the agent for a French banking house—Pioche, Bayerque and Company—representing thirty-seven million francs invested in California properties.[82] He anticipated Disneyland by a century when he built The Willows, an amusement park at Mission Dolores, just ten minutes by horsecar from downtown San Francisco, where champagne lunches were available to tired businessmen. Pioche had also invested in an electro-metallurgical works. Not content to operate in California alone, Pioche had also bought several Nevada mines. In mid-1868 he was a participant in the struggle to control the Twin River properties near Belmont.[83] Having the resources to develop any mining venture, Pioche kept agents traveling the West to locate new sources of enterprise.

When Hoffman arrived in Panaca in 1868, he found little mining activity, but a confused muddle of conflicting records pertaining to the district. The Sherwood-Vandermark party had founded the first district, closely followed by a group of California Volunteers and the Panaca residents, each party maintaining its own set of records and insisting on being the only legal claimant to the outcrops. The conflicting claims presented a bonanza in legal fees during the decade of prosperity in Pioche. Hoffman eventually purchased the claims of E. Martin Smith and began to test the rock.[84] Pioche incorporated the property in San Francisco as the Meadow Valley Company in 1869. Eventually the Sherwood-Vandermark locations were validated by the courts, since they were the original locators.

Despite Pioche's intervention in the quiescent district, the greatest share of the coming bonanza fell to John Ely and W. H. Raymond of Hiko. Both were veterans of the Pahranagat boom and had achieved positions of local prominence by 1868. Their knowledge of events among the Panaca claims, sixty miles to the east, came about as a result of their offices in county government. John Ely was a merchant in Hiko and had been appointed to the county commission in 1867.[85] W. H. Raymond was also on the commission and had been elected county recorder in November 1868, at the time that Hoffman was beginning to open the Meadow Valley Company's claims.[86] Despite Raymond's lack of success in Pahranagat, he was energetically promoting the district among eastern investors. Both men had married and were maintaining families in Hiko.[87] As recorder, Raymond would have been informed of all changes in ownership of claims in the county. Through this office Raymond learned of Pioche's interest in the Panaca claims and determined to participate in the development.

The first overt act to compete with the Meadow Valley Company came on March 10, 1869. On that date John H. Ely held a miners' meeting which revised the regulations of the Meadow Valley district and renamed the area the Ely district (no false modesty here).[88] On the same date Ely located the Pioche mine.[89] This was evidently the old Panacker shaft and later the best of the Raymond and Ely properties. Raymond's part in the transaction was to record the change in district regulations and insure that the new locations would have the sanctity of law. Since the Meadow Valley Company had few men on the claims, Ely would have needed very few miners to have a majority at the meeting, called without lengthy prior notice. Although the business was an arrogant usurpation of the customary method of altering district regulations, it was recorded legally and stood the challenge of later court action. In all these transactions, Raymond and Ely shared equally in their holdings.

The Meadow Valley Company had been operating as secretly as possible, intending to test the ores and purchase the best properties before anyone else recognized the possibilities.[90] Raymond and Ely had just the opposite intent: they needed financial backing and took every opportunity to broadcast the potential of the district. By the first weeks of April, notices began to appear in the Nevada press:

> *The Ely is a base metal district, but the ore produces from fifty to eighty per cent. of lead, which contains from $200 to $800 in silver, and assays at the rate of thousands of dollars per ton have been obtained.*[91]

The Meadow Valley Company intended to use smelters to separate the metals from barren rock. This metal would be shipped in "pigs" by wagon to Elko, then to San Francisco via the Central Pacific for treatment in Pioche's metallurgical plant.[92] Prior to the completion of the Central Pacific, none of this base ore could be worked.[93] Experimentation with the base ores of White Pine and Eureka led to the use of small, handbuilt smelters in preference to the stamp mill or Washoe Pan Process. The high percentage of lead prevented the earlier methods evolved on the Comstock to function satisfactorily.[94] By May 1868 the Meadow Valley Company had already decided to erect a smelter and had the equipment on the road by wagon from Elko.[95] In the meantime, the richer, hand-sorted ores were being shipped to San Francisco.[96] The only significant working was a forty-foot-deep shaft, appropriately named the Pioche mine.

While the Meadow Valley Company experimented with smelters, John Ely was visiting nearby districts, passing out ore samples and trying to interest others in the Ely deposits. Both he and Raymond would have sold their claims, but as no takers could be found for a district that had yet to produce bullion they realized that they would have to develop their properties. The five-stamp mill brought to Pahranagat in 1866 by Raymond was freighted to a site just north of Panaca. Supposedly, the hauling was done by Mormon farmers from Panaca, who knew John Ely through his wife and trusted him for the costs incurred. However, Ely did not put all his eggs in one basket: while he was moving Raymond's mill to what became known as Bullionville, he had a Professor Scheuner building a smelter similar to the Meadow Valley Company's small plant.[97] The

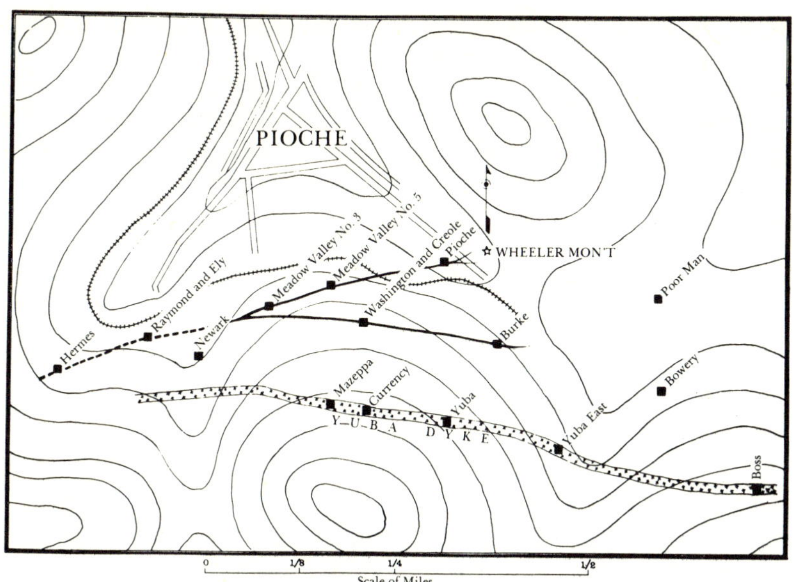

Map of Pioche and immediate vicinity, showing the relative positions of the chief mines. Reprinted from Fred J. Pack, "Geology of Pioche, Nevada, and Vicinity," *School of Mines Quarterly,* Columbia University (April and July 1906), opp. p. 371.

mill was moved in midsummer 1869. The state mineralogist visited the Ely district in August and described the mill as powered by a twelve-horsepower steam engine, feeding two agitators and four tubs.

In all the descriptions of the Ely district during 1869-70, W. H. Raymond is scarcely mentioned. Although today we usually refer to the partnership as the Raymond and Ely Company, it was consistently titled the Ely and Raymond Company by contemporaries.[98] The firm was incorporated on December 31, 1870, as the Raymond and Ely Company, however.[99] Thereafter, John Ely's name disappeared from the local newspapers; presumably he left the district for Salt Lake City, where he again entered the mercantile business.[100] That mundane occupation did not suit a man of Ely's imagination; so he exchanged the City of the Saints for the City of Light. From 1872 until 1875 Ely lived the good life in Paris and speculated in a gold venture and steamship lines to French Guiana.[101] After losing the reputed half million he took from Pioche, Ely and his wife separated; both returned destitute to Pioche in 1875.[102] A quarter century later, Ely died a pauper in Nogales, Arizona, on January 25, 1901.[103]

During all of 1869 and most of 1870, the Meadow Valley Company was the biggest operator in Pioche. The organization had capable men in the field and money to expend on development. The first working smelter was built under Charles Hoffman's direction in early 1869. By summer it was working three to four tons of the richest ore from the Pioche claims daily.[104] In July the exploratory workings on the Pioche property had penetrated the vein up to forty feet and found massive quantities of smelting ores high in lead. Based on this information, the company decided to build a large smelting plant. Two furnaces, one chloridizing and one cupelling, were shipped into the district and erected.[105] The work went slowly and the smelter was not ready for use until February or March of 1870. At approximately the same time that the costly smelter was completed, underground exploration made it obsolete.

As crews worked deeper into the Pioche claims, they broke through the capping of lead-rich silver ore into rock that could be milled by the much cheaper Washoe Pan Process. The free-milling ore existed in chimneys, more than forty-odd feet below the surface. These chimneys of less complex ore alternated with similar chimneys of smelting rock in most of the mines of both the Meadow Valley Company and its competitors. Samples of the free and base ores were sent to Louis Janin, a metallurgist in Hamilton, for tests. Janin found a means of combining the two grades of ore and working them in a modified Washoe Pan process. The base ores were roasted prior to being mixed with the free rock; then the silver was extracted to about eighty percent of total value.[106] Janin's twenty-stamp mill was shipped from Elko in April 1870 and fired up on July 15 in Dry Valley. After some experimentation with chemicals and other additives to the process, Janin was able to provide the Meadow Valley Company with a reliable separation facility for their already proven ore.

Despite its predominance in the district, the Meadow Valley Company was not the first to perfect a milling process. John Ely had taken options on the claims held by the Panaca settlers and bonded others as well.[107] In summer 1869 Raymond's mill had been brought to Bullionville, where desultory attempts were made to work ore from the Raymond and Ely claims near the Panacker shaft. These failed, however, because of the high percentage of lead. In the fall Charles Gracey, an expatriate from White Pine, persuaded Ely to let him experiment with the mill. Gracey chose to work ores from the Burke mine, a claim Ely had bonded earlier.[108] These must have been taken from the surface, but even so were free-milling. The contamination problem experienced by the Meadow Valley Company did not extend to the Burke claims. In January, Gracey was able to get the mill ready for the first run. The amalgamation method proved successful and the Raymond and Ely Company was shipping silver bricks.[109] All the work had been done by local miners and farmers on credit. It is a testament to John Ely's gift of "jawbone," joined with a great deal of luck and coincidence, that the right combination of equipment and men occurred in a remote part of southeastern Nevada at precisely the right time.

The regular shipment of bullion by the Raymond and Ely Company, at a rate of $500 to $800 per day, brought a typical "rush" to Pioche. The White Pine area was declining and provided most of the early arrivals. Once the masses of ore known to exist underground had been proved valuable, Pioche began to assume the lawless aspects that have characterized accounts of the district ever since.[110]

5. Mormon-Gentile Struggle for Mastery

Though this is not a study of the Pioche or other southeastern Nevada mining booms, the emphasis on mining is necessary to illustrate how the rural character and LDS control of the area were gradually eroded. The catalyst for this change was the discovery of exploitable mineral deposits. Thus far, the effect of the Pahranagat boom and the initial discovery of the Pioche outcrops had been to move the mining frontier from central Nevada to the Meadow Valley region and bring about direct contact with the Mormon barrier line established by policy of the First Presidency of the Church in 1864-65. The terminal portion of this paper is a description of the struggle for control of those areas and the alternatives for the inhabitants, both LDS and gentile.

More than a year was required to establish a county government for Lincoln County following the federal cession of parts of Arizona and Utah territories to Nevada on May 5, 1866. The Nevada Legislature created Lincoln County in response to the discovery of silver at Pahranagat in February 1866 and incorporated into the act a clause to include any territory later added to the state contiguous to its borders. Even so, the slow arrival of the appointees to office prevented formation of the county apparatus until late April 1867.[111]

The refusal of the LDS settlements in Meadow Valley and along the Muddy to acknowledge the change in sovereignty precipitated a clash that was not resolved until the eastern border of Nevada was surveyed four years later.[112] Prior to 1869 there was not sufficient reason for the county to exercise its authority over Mormon ranchers. Indeed, there was good political reason to let the situation remain in the status quo: first, the tax revenues gained from assessments on the subsistence farms would never pay for the litigation required; second, there was every evidence to show that the Mormons would vote

Democratic and pose a threat to the elected officeholders at Hiko, who were Black Republican.[113] Faced with that dire possibility, especially since the loss of mining population in 1867 and 1868 gave the Mormons numerical supremacy, the politicians of Hiko quietly ignored the eviction of the county assessor from Meadow Valley and waited for the boundary survey to settle the problem. There is good reason to suspect that the Hiko officeholders would have been content to let the situation drift indefinitely had the Pioche boom failed.[114] The split in loyalty in the newly acquired region was clearly divided by religion: the gentile miners of El Dorado Canyon began to register their claims in the new county seat, while the LDS settlements were too preoccupied with the problems of survival to turn a responsive face to the appeals from Hiko.[115] These efforts to persuade the Mormons that they were indeed a part of Nevada would have been inconsequential if the Panaca deposits had proved barren.

The Meadow Valley settlements prospered because of their nearby markets in Pahranagat and the mining camps of central Nevada. Panaca reportedly had more than five hundred inhabitants by the end of 1868, making it the largest single community in Lincoln County.[116] Property there was assessed as a part of Washington County, Utah, and taxes were paid regularly at the Utah rate. Taxes in Utah were payable in kind, which helped the specie-poor residents of Meadow Valley. The Lincoln County assessor made a token appearance in 1867 but was ignored.[117] Other Lincoln County officials made visits but were no more successful than the assessor. Meadow Valley's contempt for the edict of Lincoln County was pointedly ignored until January 1870.

In that month two important events took place: Gracey's process succeeded in freeing silver from the Burke rock, and complaints against fifty-nine families for nonpayment of taxes were filed in justice court.[118] There is a direct link between the two seemingly unrelated occurrences. When the Meadow Valley Company began its attempts to develop the Panaca claims, the farms along the valley appreciated in value. Should the claims prove valuable, then the market for farm produce would grow correspondingly. The gentile population of Hiko, hungry enough in any case after two years of *borrasca* in Pahranagat, had been through enough mining booms to recognize that fortunes were made in merchandising as well as mining. They began to look for ways to preempt the Panaca farms and occupy the valley themselves should a boom occur. By January 1870 they had their excuse and undertook to attach the properties in the name of the county and sell them at sheriff's sale.

After transferal of the case to the district court, the hearing was postponed until the boundary survey, then in progress, had been carried south far enough to determine if Meadow Valley was in the state as alleged.[119] On December 19, 1870, St. George Church authorities officially informed the Panaca residents by letter that their homes were in Nevada. The residents were allowed to decide individually whether they would stay or leave. By this time, the Pioche boom was well under way and the Mormons of Panaca more than shared in the flush times. The overwhelming majority elected to stay and fight the tax problem through the courts. A year later, the county commission decided to withdraw its action for collection of back taxes. After five years of dispute, the threat of legal collection had been resolved.

It is interesting to speculate as to the motives of the commission in absolving the Panaca residents. The Pioche community was wholly anti-Mormon and could be depended upon to empanel a jury that would find for the county; in fact, in the only case that went to trial over the tax issue, the jury's decision was thrown out of court by the district judge, Mortimer Fuller, because of prejudice toward the Mormon defendants.[120] The most plausible explanation for the commission's decision was that the Panacans were no longer feared by the neighbor community of Pioche. The population of Pioche reached an approximate five thousand by 1872, about ten times that of Panaca.[121] The bloc of votes from Panaca was more than offset by the miners of Pioche. Even more important, the Panacans were content to return home at the end of the working day and ignore the internecine squabbles of the mining companies and politicians. They wisely refused to become committed to one faction or the other. There is nothing more desired in a neighbor.

To an extent, propinquity alleviated the xenophobia of both groups. The Mormons were engaged in many of the most necessary occupations. They marketed produce, sold meat, hauled freight, and did not compete with the gentile miner underground. In general, they were as wholeheartedly materialistic as their gentile acquaintances. One can forget that a neighbor has several wives if he resembles you in other outward appearances and common values. After several years of armed truce, the Panaca community came to be regarded as a group of backward, slightly distasteful relatives, but allowed to exist. On their part, the Panacans never raised issues that would threaten the political hegemony of Pioche and raise the specter of "witch-hunting" or arrests for plural marriage.

On the practical side, the county commission probably considered the costs of fighting the tax issue through the supreme court of the state. Any local decision would certainly be appealed. The case of the defendants was good: they had consistently paid their assessments to Washington County, Utah, during the dispute, and Lincoln County had frequently announced that it would let the matter rest until the boundary survey had been run.[122] The question was over back taxes, not the future assessments. The commissioners compromised and the Panacans quietly paid the 1872 and subsequent assessments.

The ultimate decision in the Muddy region was not as simple as at Panaca. The reasons for colonization along the Muddy and Virgin rivers had been strategic rather than economic. The First Presidency's policy of occupying any arable lands between the older Utah towns and the advancing mining frontier required that the malarial swamps of the Muddy be settled before they could be taken by others. There were no markets nearby for these colonists to exchange their produce for specie. Nevertheless, missionaries were named in Salt Lake City during the general conference in October 1864 and arrived the following January to clear fields and begin a settlement.

The reputation of the Muddy Mission was the worst of the outlying pioneer villages. An attempt to colonize, begun in

1858, had been abandoned; but the threat of gentile occupation forced the Church authorities to reconsider. Tenure on the Muddy was a real test of the commitment of any member. Even the *Deseret News* was forced to admit openly the general opinion held by members:

> *The general idea prevailing in Salt Lake about the Muddy is, that it is a sort of purgatory or place of punishment. . . . This is doubtless the case with some people who have left the long settled portions of Utah reluctantly.*[123]

As stories of heat, sickness, Indians, and hardship spread among the faithful in Utah, members held their collective breath as the names of those selected to go south were read during each general conference. Many settlers, well over half, took less than a year to abandon the mission and return to Utah. A constant stream of replacements had to be named yearly to keep the settlements alive. One would-be missionary "fainted at the news; everyone knew of the blistering alkali desert and had no wish to go."[124] Another commented that "many had been called to go to 'Dixie' but to the Muddy was much worse."[125] The best example of the low regard for the Muddy occurred in 1867, when the pope was forced from Rome by Italian revolutionaries. U.S. Secretary of State Seward offered His Holiness asylum in the United States; the Mormons reacted by caustically offering a farm on the Muddy for the papal entourage, should they wish to emigrate to Utah:

> *The telegrams say that Seward has invited the Pope to take refuge in America. A few days ago we offered his Holiness a farm on the Muddy or some good place in this Territory. Will he accept?*[126]

One senses an inference that the Muddy was the ultimate in earthly damnation that could be provided Pius IX.

The settlements barely kept alive; the warehousing center of Callville, which might have been a market for their produce, never developed and was abandoned. Traffic along the Old

Spanish Trail decreased as the Union Pacific crossed Utah. Floods, drought, Indian attack, and persistent sickness occurred one after the other. Travelers passing through the area rarely failed to comment on the abject poverty exhibited by the residents. Still, some families hung on.

The First Presidency recognized that the Muddy area was part of Arizona in 1864. The Second Arizona Territorial Legislature created Pah-Ute County to include the LDS settlements on December 22, 1865. Earlier, all of Arizona north and west of the Colorado River had been part of Mohave County, one of the original four subdivisions of Arizona Territory. The reason for the division of the county in December 1865 was to provide a separate government for the LDS settlements. Earlier in the same year, the Utah Territorial Legislature had memorialized Congress, asking for the area north of the Colorado River and east of the thirty-eighth meridian. This cession would have given Utah all the land between St. George and Las Vegas Wash.

In February 1869 the Utah Territorial Legislature created Rio Virgen County, centered on the Muddy villages. The step may have been taken in an effort to strengthen the tie to Utah and aid the settlers in their conflict with Nevada. During the same month that Rio Virgen County was established, Nevada, chronically in need of revenue, enacted a statute requiring tax payment in coin.[127] This requirement posed no hardship for the Meadow Valley residents, but the Muddy settlements had far less access to specie and had to endure a drought in 1869.

Crisis on the Muddy

By 1870 affairs along the Muddy had reached a critical phase. The Meadow Valley-Callville barrier line was failing as the Panaca claims underwent intensive testing by F. L. A. Pioche and his associates, while completion of the transcontinental railroad had negated the need for a port on the Colorado River. The colony on the Muddy had maintained itself only through infusion of fresh members and continual shipments of supplies from Utah. To continue the colony as a means of denying the area to non-LDS settlers seemed futile, since no competition had developed in the five years since 1865.

The First Presidency's decision on the future of the colony seems to have been reached in 1870. In an effort to study the problem firsthand, President Young made an almost unprecedented two trips to this isolated settlement.[128] His experience with the mission had come only through second-party accounts; the necessity of deciding whether to terminate or continue the mission caused him to assess conditions personally.

President Young spent the middle portion of March 1870 in the valley. What he saw convinced him that conditions were totally unsatisfactory for the self-sufficient agricultural community typical in Utah.[129] However, the decision was held until the survey had determined whether the valley was in Nevada or Utah.

The survey was performed under contract by a Carson City engineer, Isaac James, who began work in late September. A party of about fifteen men, well armed because of local Indian raids, began surveying at the Central Pacific tracks and went north to the Idaho border, then south to the Colorado. The job was completed in mid-December 1870.[130]

The word reached St. George early in December that the Meadow Valley and Muddy settlements were in Nevada. Immediately, apparently without time for planning, messages were sent to the affected missions explaining the situation. The timing indicates that the decision to retain the Meadow Valley area and abandon the Muddy villages may have been made before December and held until it was certain that the southern settlements were in Nevada. Even so, the Muddy settlers themselves had to decide whether to terminate their stay in the mission.[131]

Because of the sensitive situation, Joseph W. Young, a nephew of President Young, was sent with the official letter to explain the wishes of the First Presidency. The letter was carefully framed to explain the possible dangers to the settlers should they choose to remain in Nevada; indeed, the pejorative elements were overstressed. High taxes, lack of markets, and the "unscrupulous character of many of the officers" were all enumerated as reasons suitable for leaving the valley. Meetings were held in the three wards on December 20-21, 1870, and a resolution was prepared stating that the mission was abandoned "for reasons expressed in the Epistle of President Brigham Young and other reasons."[132]

Why was the Muddy abandoned and Meadow Valley retained? The reasons offered by President Young to justify leaving the Muddy apply equally to Meadow Valley, with the exception of markets. But even when the Pioche boom was two years in the future, Panaca was thriving. Those "other reasons" cited by Bishop Stark in his resolution announcing the abandonment of the Muddy were the real causes of leaving the valley. Succinctly put, the colony was not self-sustaining and the colonists were in desperate straits. When the opportunity was given to leave, only Daniel Bonelli and his family voted to stay; Bonelli was supposedly in a state of apostasy and a member of the New Movement within the Church.[133] He refused to abandon his improvements and is reported to have maintained later that "the Church left him, he didn't leave the Church."[134] At the same meetings that voted for termination of the colony, petitions were drawn asking the Nevada legislature to grant the settlements county status and cancellation of back taxes. The petitions were carried to Carson City by O. D. Gass of Las Vegas but were never considered. The colonists left by February 20, 1871.

The idea that county officers persecuted the Muddy settlers has been promulgated right to the present. Popular articles on local history appearing in southern Nevada newspapers consistently present this picture of a heroic band of dedicated missionaries being forced from their homes by rapacious sheriffs and tax assessors.

Scholarly attention to the situation has stressed the problem of tax payment with specie. Elbert Edwards comes closest to citing the low morale and infighting among the missionaries.[135] Bonelli, in his letter to the *Salt Lake Tribune* explaining why the mission was terminated, said that the increase in taxes would be minimal and the settlers could have paid had they desired to stay.[136] Corbett studied the tax rates of both Arizona and Nevada and concluded that the increase would approach a factor of three.[137] The best argument to the tax problem is the experience of those who stayed: Bonelli prospered in Rioville, and the Panaca residents thrived as they participated in the Pioche boom. Had the Muddy farms been able to produce a surplus, it could have been marketed in Pioche. The feeling of some Muddy residents was no doubt expressed by a boy who "admitted touching a match to it [his family's adobe house] so they couldn't go back. He wanted to go where schools were, and people, and where his mother wouldn't have to work so hard."[138]

6. Conclusions

Southeastern Nevada, that area now comprising Clark and Lincoln counties, had little attraction for permanent settlers until mineral discoveries were made. The Pioche and Pahranagat districts drew attention from Nevada politicians who imagined profit to themselves from the deposits if they could insure that the areas were firmly in the state. The result was partial dismemberment of Utah and Arizona territories, as Congress yielded to the demands of Nevada in exchange for her votes.

The rising number of miners visiting the Panaca claims in 1864, with clear intent to settle and work the deposits, posed a threat to Utah's religiously segregated communities. A whole series of countermeasures brought missionaries into Meadow Valley, along the Virgin and Muddy rivers, and caused a warehouse center to be built on the Colorado. These steps, all taken in 1864, created a barrier to Utah that was hopefully impenetrable by the mining frontier pushing east from Nevada. Further, the long-standing proscription against mining was quietly withdrawn in 1864-65, as LDS guides and support were provided to friendly prospectors in order to survey the mineral potential of southwest Utah.

One of these joint efforts at prospecting located the Pahranagat deposits in 1865 and brought a minor boom to the doorstep of Meadow Valley. Actual competition between Mormon and gentile settlers was postponed until 1869, when the Pioche district became active. In that area a pattern emerged: whenever a mining discovery was made, the LDS barrier failed. The non-LDS settlers flocked in, regardless of the control of water or land by the Saints. Mormon claims to mining properties were voided by the courts. Coexistence in Meadow Valley was possible as long as the Panaca residents limited themselves to nonmining economic activities. A political compromise was effected in 1871 that exchanged suits for back taxes for assurances that the gentile political hegemony would not be threatened.

The final act in the political compromise was abandonment of the Muddy settlements. Even before the Nevada-Utah boundary was surveyed in 1871, the Muddy mission was in difficulty; it required constant resupply and new missionaries. The living conditions were recognized to be particularly harsh, and the anti-Mormon *Salt Lake Tribune* advertised it as a Siberia for troublemakers from the more favorable valleys in the north. Even so, abandonment of the mission was delayed until the government survey had shown the settlements to be in Nevada. The taxes of Nevada, much higher than in Utah, and the threat of sheriff's sale, were used to justify the decision of the First Presidency. The settlers themselves bore the responsibility of electing to leave.

By early 1871, the political and economic structure was fixed in southern Nevada. A gentile government was predominant. Mormon residents, although not evicted from their property or given higher tax assessments, had abandoned one area and thrived in another. So long as there was no clear-cut challenge to the status quo, each group tolerated the other. Social segregation between the two participating elements was strictly enforced by peer group pressures. This social and political arrangement became a precedent for later gentile-LDS confrontations in Utah. Earlier the LDS Church had fled from persecution; now it could go no farther. It had to find a means of living with its fellow citizens. A viable compromise was found in southeastern Nevada, and the experience was taken to a growing number of localities as the mining and transportation frontiers passed successively through Utah.

Notes

1. Ruth Lee and Sylvia Wadsworth, *A Century in Meadow Valley: 1864-1964* (Salt Lake City: Deseret News Press, 1966), pp.1-4.

2. *Deseret News*, June 22, 1864, p. 304. Both the *News* and the *Salt Lake Daily Telegraph* were Church newspapers. Mining events were rarely reported, and then accompanied by adverse comment.

3. *Mining and Scientific Press*, October 28, 1865, p. 264.

4. *Pioche Daily Record*, March 29, 1873, p. 3. The best account of Hamblin's first trip to Pioche is found in a letter from Edward Bunker to Brigham Young, January 20, 1864, found in the Papers of Brigham Young, Church Archives, The Church of Jesus Christ of Latter-day Saints, Salt Lake City: "For some time past the Indians have persuaded him [Hamblin] to go with them to a lead mine as they said the Mormons wanted lead. Last fall he consented to go with them. He found the mine situated about 12 miles from Meadow valley lying about northwest from here and about 120 miles distant." Sample bits of ore assayed 10-15% silver. Drought in "Dixie" during 1863 made several of the southern Utah residents anxious to move into the valleys close to the silver strike. President Young was asked to approve the move.

5. The *Raymond and Ely v. Hermes* suit was one of the most important pieces of litigation ever held in Pioche. It was marked by bribery, fraud, and perjured testimony.

6. James W. Hulse, *Lincoln County, Nevada: 1864-1909*, Nevada Studies in History and Political Science No. 10 (Reno: University of Nevada Press, 1971), pp.6-7. The center point for the district seems to be in dispute. Vandermark, during the 1873 lawsuit, said it was the discovery stake at the Panaca claim. Others chose the Panaca Spring.

7. *Pioche Daily Record*, March 29, 1873, p. 3; March 30, 1873, p. 3.

8. Ibid., March 28, 1873, p. 3. Hamblin never lived to enjoy his discoveries. It is believed that he was poisoned over ownership of some claims. See Bill Vincent, "Spring Valley in the Early Days," *The Nevadan Magazine* (in) *Las Vegas Review-Journal*, June 23, 1968, p. 24.

9. Brigham Young to Edward Bunker, February 6, 1864. Papers of Brigham Young, Church Archives. Bunker was "to claim, survey and

take off as soon as possible, those veins of ore that Br. Hamblin is aware of, and that you mention in your letter. . . ." Erastus Snow was in Salt Lake City at the time news of the discovery was received and returned with a book of mining regulations.

10. *Mining and Scientific Press,* December 24, 1864, p. 412. The tone of this article demonstrates how the discovery alone was able to cause influential citizens to dream of "another Comstock" in the wilds of southern Nevada. The possibility of this gentile intrusion caused alarm in Salt Lake City.

11. Milton R. Hunter, "The Mormons and the Colorado River," *American Historical Review,* 44 (April 1939): 241. Hunter and later students of the Colorado River settlements stress the motive of cheaper transportation when discussing the reasons behind Brigham Young's decision to extend his settlements to the southwest.

12. *American Journal of Mining,* May 12, 1866, p. 100.

13. Hulse, *Lincoln County,* p. 13; R. H. Stretch, *Annual Report of the State Mineralogist for the State of Nevada for 1866* (Carson City: State Printer, 1867), pp. 64-65; James Graves Scrugham, ed., *Nevada: A Narrative of the Conquest of a Frontier Land; Comprising the Story of Her People from the Dawn of History to the Present Time* (Chicago: The American Historical Society, 1935), 1:615; Myron Angel, ed., *History of Nevada. With Illustrations and Biographical Sketches of Its Prominent Men and Pioneers* (Oakland: Thompson and West, 1881), pp. 477, 485.

14. Report of Dr. A. Blatchly, Mining Engineer, to J. Ross Browne, Special Commissioner for the Collection of Mining Statistics, Austin, Nevada, November 26, 1866, *A Report upon the Mineral Resources of the States and Territories West of the Rocky Mountains* (Washington, D.C.: Government Printing Office, 1867), p. 134.

15. *Mining and Scientific Press,* September 23, 1865, p. 182. This was not the only contact between Day and Governor Blasdel. In the spring of 1866, Day was a member of a party of miners that rescued the governor when he was trying to reach Pahranagat from Carson City.

16. Ibid., August 11, 1866, p. 87. William Henry Raymond spent time in Pahranagat in late 1865, purchased bonds on various claims, then went to New York City to raise capital to develop the properties. *Territorial Enterprise,* January 27, 1867, p. 2.

17. Speech of Utah Territorial Representative William H. Hooper, *Congressional Globe,* May 3, 1866, pp. 2369-70. This speech was followed

by Arizona's territorial representative, John N. Goodwin, who outlined Arizona's objections.

18. Donald Bufkin, "The Lost County of Pah-Ute," *Arizoniana,* 5 (Summer 1964): 1-12; Elbert Edwards, "Southern Nevada's Centennial January 18, 1967," *The Nevadan Magazine* (in) *Las Vegas Review-Journal,* January 15, 1967, pp. 3-6; John M. Townley, "The Hiko Silver Strike Spurred Annexation," *Sunday Scene Magazine* (in) *Las Vegas Sun,* August 2, 1970, p. 7; Hulse, *Lincoln County,* p. 16.

19. *Report of the Surveyor-General and Land Register of the State of Nevada* (in) *Appendix to the Legislative Journal, 14th Session* (Carson City: State Printer, 1889), p. 15. Arizona had claimed that the cession of land was never constitutionally accepted by the state of Nevada.

20. *American Journal of Mining,* August 22, 1868, p. 114.

21. Hulse, *Lincoln County,* p. 8, citing Andrew Karl Larson, *I Was Called to Dixie: The Virgin River Basin: Unique Experiences in Mormon Pioneering* (Salt Lake City: The Deseret News Press, 1961), p. 162, and *Deseret News,* June 14, 1865.

The letters in the papers of Brigham Young, Church Archives, have several references to the early 1864 decision to permit Church members in Meadow Valley to locate claims on the Panaca ledge. Compare Erastus Snow to Brigham Young, March 28, 1864:

> *The Clara brethren have taken possession of the lead and silver Mines near Meadow valley with the view of holding claim and working them only as wisdom may direct;*

and Erastus Snow to Brigham Young, March 1, 1864:

> *The Clara brethren have made a move for settling Clover Valley and covering the mines in that region as you suggested.*

The dispensation did not last. The individualism created by participation in mining soon threatened the cohesion of the settlements, and President Erastus Snow found it necessary to instruct his bishops to cut off from the Church those persons who continued to work mining claims.

22. Hulse, *Lincoln County,* pp. 15-16. Blasdel had asked Ely by letter for information and may have offered to bond some claims. There were other communications between Blasdel and Eastern investors.

23. *Appendix "E" to the Annual Report of the State Mineralogist of the State of Nevada for 1866* (in) *Journal of the Senate during the Third*

Session of the Legislature of the State of Nevada, 1867 (Carson City: State Printer, 1867), pp. 141-47. This diary of the trip was kept by H. L. Stretch and records the difficulties of crossing the hitherto unexplored deserts between Death Valley and Pahranagat.

24. *American Journal of Mining,* July 21, 1866, pp. 259-60; *Mining and Scientific Press,* November 3, 1866, p. 279. After his return from Pahranagat, Governor Durkee kept a pair of large samples of bullion on his desk. He returned during the summer a second time.

25. *Weekly Union Vedette,* April 5, 1866, p. 4.

26. Angel, *History of Nevada,* pp. 187, 347; *Deseret News,* April 12, 1866, p. 152.

27. *Pioche Weekly Record,* March 6, 1886, p. 3; U.S. Bureau of the Census, *Lincoln County, Nevada Manuscript Census 1870, Bullionville Section,* p. 2.

28. Angel, *History of Nevada,* pp. 186-87. *Silver Bend Reporter,* November 23, 1867, p. 3.

29. *Mining and Scientific Press,* April 28, 1866, p. 257.

30. *American Journal of Mining,* June 16, 1866, p. 180.

31. *Mining and Scientific Press,* September 8, 1866, p. 151.

32. *Territorial Enterprise,* January 27, 1867, p. 2.

33. *Mining and Scientific Press,* August 25, 1866, p. 151.

34. Ibid., August 18, 1866, p. 103.

35. *American Journal of Mining,* September 8, 1866, p. 372.

36. *Los Angeles News,* June 29, 1866, p. 2.

37. *Territorial Enterprise,* January 24, 1867, p. 3; January 27, 1867, p. 2.

38. *Mining and Scientific Press,* April 27, 1867, p. 263. The notes circulated among residents as a medium of exchange.

39. *American Journal of Mining,* November 17, 1866, p. 115.

40. Ibid., March 2, 1867, p. 356. Hamblin later guided a party from Pahranagat through the Grand Canyon and to the sources of the Grand River. Like his brother Jacob, William Hamblin was evidently occupied with frequent exploring missions for LDS authorities.

41. *Territorial Enterprise,* February 1, 1867, p. 3.

42. *American Journal of Mining,* October 20, 1866, p. 58.

43. Ibid., May 11, 1867, pp. 125-26.

44. *Silver Bend Reporter,* August 17, 1867, p. 3.

45. *Mining and Scientific Press,* February 9, 1867, p. 87.

46. *Silver Bend Reporter,* August 3, 1867, p. 3.

47. *Territorial Enterprise,* January 27, 1867, p. 2; *Mining and Scientific Press,* February 16, 1867, p. 112; *American Journal of Mining,* February 23, 1867, p. 338.

48. *Daily Reese River Reveille,* June 8, 1867, p. 1.

49. Ibid., October 18, 1867, p.1.

50. *Silver Bend Reporter,* September 7, 1867, p. 3.

51. Ibid., August 17, 1867, p. 3.

52. *Daily Reese River Reveille,* June 8, 1867, p. 1.

53. *Silver Bend Reporter,* June 22, 1867, p. 3.

54. Ibid., August 31, 1867, p. 2.

55. *Daily Reese River Reveille,* January 17, 1868, p. 1.

56. Ibid., May 8, 1868, p. 1.

57. Ibid., May 13, 1868, p. 1.

58. *American Journal of Mining,* July 25, 1868, p. 59.

59. *Engineering and Mining Journal,* November 23, 1869, p. 324.

60. Ibid., December 7, 1869, pp. 356-57.

61. *Daily Reese River Reveille,* March 17, 1868, p. 1.

62. Ibid., August 10, 1867, p. 2.

63. Ibid., March 17, 1868, p. 1.

64. *American Journal of Mining,* July 4, 1868, p. 4.

65. *Silver Bend Reporter,* September 7, 1867, p. 3.

66. Charles S. Cotton, "Early Days in Nevada," in pamphlet, *Side Lights on the Civil War; Early Days in Nevada* (Cowansville, Quebec: Cotton's Cooperative Publishing Co., April 1912), pp. 24-25.

67. *American Journal of Mining,* May 12, 1866, p. 100.

68. Ibid., August 18, 1866, p. 324.

69. *Silver Bend Reporter,* June 8, 1867, p. 2.

70. *Mining and Scientific Press,* November 24, 1866, p. 334; *American Journal of Mining,* September 8, 1866, p. 372.

71. Stretch, *Annual Report of the State Mineralogist,* p. 66. Stretch first uses the term *Hico* to identify the settlement.

72. *Mining and Scientific Press,* December 15, 1866, p. 375.

73. *Daily Reese River Reveille,* August 3, 1867, p. 2.

74. *Silver Bend Reporter,* October 5, 1867, p. 2.

75. Angel, *History of Nevada,* pp. 342-43. John M. Townley, "Hiko Hangs Its Horsethieves," *Sunday Scene Magazine* (in) *Las Vegas Sun,* December 7, 1969, p. 16.

76. *Daily Reese River Reveille,* April 6, 1868, p. 1; Angel, *History of Nevada,* p. 348.

77. *Silver Bend Reporter,* September 7, 1867, p. 3.

78. *Territorial Enterprise,* April 14, 1869, p. 3.

79. *Daily Reese River Reveille,* November 23, 1870, p. 2.

80. *Biennial Report of the State Mineralogist, 1871-1872* (Carson City: State Printer, 1873), p. 84.

81. Scrugham, *Nevada: A Narrative,* 1:615.

82. *San Francisco Daily Herald,* November 7, 1857, p. 2.

83. *Mountain Champion,* June 3, 1868, p. 3.

84. Hulse, *Lincoln County,* p. 9.

85. U.S. Works Progress Administration, Historical Records Survey, *Lincoln County Commission Record,* p. 10.

86. *Mountain Champion,* November 28, 1868, p. 3.

87. U.S. Bureau of the Census, *Lincoln County, Nevada, Manuscript Census, 1870, Bullionville Section,* pp. 1-2.

88. A. F. White, *Annual Report of the State Mineralogist of the State of Nevada for 1869 and 1870* (in) *Appendix to the Senate Journal, 4th Session* (Carson City: State Printer, 1871), pp. 101-2.

89. Ibid.

90. *Territorial Enterprise,* July 2, 1869, p. 3. "We have here a company, lately incorporated in San Francisco, under the name of the Meadow Valley Mining Company, operating as secretly as possible, trying to keep out other companies and miners until they have grabbed all the best ledges."

91. *Mining and Scientific Press,* April 24, 1869, p. 263.

92. Ibid., November 6, 1869, p. 295.

93. *Engineering and Mining Journal,* August 30, 1870, p. 138.

94. R. W. Raymond, *Statistics of Mines and Mining in the States and Territories West of the Rocky Mountains for the Year 1870* (Washington, D.C.: Government Printing Office, 1872), p. 164.

95. *Daily Inland Empire,* May 23, 1869, p. 3.

96. *Engineering and Mining Journal,* November 23, 1869, p. 325. Six thousand pounds of ore, supposedly worth $18,000, had been shipped.

The source given was the town of "Pioche." Evidently by late 1869 the town was known by the name of its leading promoter.

97. *Daily Reese River Reveille,* October 21, 1869, p. 3.

98. See the Nevada Mining News section of either *Engineering and Mining Journal* or *Mining and Scientific Press.*

99. *Mining and Scientific Press,* January 14, 1871, p. 21.

100. *Lincoln County Record,* February 1, 1901, p. 4.

101. *Pioche Weekly Record,* March 6, 1886, p. 3.

102. *Eureka Daily Sentinel,* June 23, 1875, p. 2; *Daily Elko Independent,* November 8, 1875, p. 2.

103. *Tuscarora Times-Review,* January 29, 1901, p. 3; *White Pine News,* January 31, 1901, p. 1; Alfred Merritt Smith, *Resources Report: White Pine County, Nevada, 1958* (Washington, D.C.: Government Printing Office, 1958), pp. 8-9.

104. *Mining and Scientific Press,* July 10, 1869, p. 23.

105. Ibid., November 6, 1869, p. 295.

106. Raymond, *Statistics of Mines,* pp. 164-65.

107. *Daily Territorial Enterprise,* March 23, 1870, p. 1. "He is a king-bee among the Mormons, and most of the old titles to mines located by persons of that persuasion have fallen into his possession."

108. *Daily Reese River Reveille,* February 19, 1870, p. 1.

109. Hulse, *Lincoln County,* p. 19.

110. *Daily Reese River Reveille,* February 19, 1870, p. 1. Less than a month after Raymond and Ely first shipped bullion, General Patrick Connor went to Pioche to get jumpers out of his claims and workings.

Mining and Scientific Press, February 12, 1870, p. 101. Mine owners were hiring gunmen early. A stageload of men "with Henry rifles" was reported leaving Hamilton on February 2, 1870.

111. *Territorial Enterprise,* May 18, 1867, p. 2.

112. *Daily Reese River Reveille,* December 20, 1867, p. 2.

113. *Silver Bend Reporter,* May 9, 1868, p. 2.

114. Ibid., December 28, 1867, p. 2.

115. Ibid.

116. Lee and Wadsworth, *A Century in Meadow Valley,* p. 7.

117. *Report of the State Surveyor-General of the State of Nevada* (in) *Appendix to the Senate Journal* (Carson City: State Printer, 1869), p. 148; Darius Salem Clement, *Diaries,* Church Archives, Folder 2, July 24, 1869: "Nevada had made another attempt to assess the settlements on the Muddy. A man by the name of Carlow, who formerly belonged to the Church, and known to some of our citizens, was sent for that purpose."

118. Lee and Wadsworth, *A Century in Meadow Valley,* p. 10. The chapter entitled "The Boundary Tax Dispute" was written by Barbara Mathews and is extremely well researched.

119. Ibid., p. 12.

120. Ibid., p. 14.

121. Hulse, *Lincoln County,* p. 22.

122. *Lincoln County Grand Jury Report,* submitted to the Honorable Charles G. Hubbard, Judge of the Ninth Judicial District of Nevada (Hiko) by A. W. Geer, foreman, dated December 5, 1867, given in Hiko.

123. *Deseret News,* April 14, 1869, p. 109; Brigham Young to William H. Dame, William S. Warren, and Hy Lunt, March 2, 1865, Papers of Brigham Young, Church Archives: "We are desirous of having every eligible spot on the Muddy, Los [*sic*] Vegas and the Colorado taken up by our brethren, so as to prevent stragglers who are drifting around that country, from securing land."

124. Arabell Lee Hafner (comp.), *100 Years on the Muddy* (Springville, Utah: Art City Publishing Company, 1967), p. 59; Journal History of The Church of Jesus Christ of Latter-day Saints, Church Archives, July 22, 1869, p. 2. Meadow Valley and the Muddy settlements were described as "being so far separated from the other settlements of Washington and Iron counties and forming the frontier line . . ." This shows that the communities were considered a barrier by Church authorities.

125. Hafner, *100 Years on the Muddy,* p. 66.

126. *Salt Lake Daily Telegraph,* November 3, 1867, p. 3.

127. Donald Bufkin, "The Lost County of Pah-Ute," *Arizoniana,* 5, no. 2 (Summer 1964): 9-10.

128. Hafner, *100 Years on the Muddy,* pp. 50, 87; L. A. Fleming, "The Settlements on the Muddy," *Utah Historical Quarterly*, 35, no. 2 (Spring 1967): 166, 168.

129. Georgia Lewis, "On the Muddy: The Early Settlement," *The Nevadan Magazine* (in) *Las Vegas Review-Journal,* June 20, 1970, p. 29.

130. *Territorial Enterprise,* September 14, 1870, p. 3; November 30, 1870, p. 3.

131. Hafner, *100 Years on the Muddy,* pp. 39, 71; *Daily Reese River Reveille,* March 21, 1871, p. 2.

132. Hafner, *100 Years on the Muddy,* pp. 79-81. The Muddy settlers were well aware that they could leave the mission. A letter from Erastus Snow, president of the Southern Utah Mission, dated September 17, 1870, authorized missionaries to leave at their convenience. See *Southern Utah Mission Historical Record,* St. George Stake, Book A, p. 36, HDC.

133. Pearson Starr Corbett, "A History of the Muddy Mission" (Master's thesis, Brigham Young University, 1968), p. 157.

134. Interview with R. F. Perkins, Director of the Overton Museum, April 9, 1970.

135. Elbert Edwards, "Early Mormon Settlements in Southern Nevada," *Nevada Historical Society Quarterly,* 8 (Spring 1965): 39. Violent disputes over land between "old" and "new" settlers kept the mission too chaotic for customary management by Church authorities.

136. *Daily Reese River Reveille,* March 21, 1871, p. 2.

137. Corbett, "A History of the Muddy Mission," pp. 145-49.

138. Hafner, *100 Years on the Muddy,* p. 58.

Index